AFRICAN GRE

AS PET

BEGINNERS GUIDE TO THEIR CARE, FEEDING, OWNERSHIP, BEHAVIOR, AND THEIR WONDERFUL NATURE AS PET

MICK HANSEN

Copyright© 2025 **MICK HANSEN**

All rights reserved. No part of this work may be reproduced, distributed, or transmitted in any form or by any means, including photocopying, recording, or other electronic or mechanical methods without the prior written permission of the publisher

Table of Contents

CHAPTER 1 5

The Intelligent Companion – Understanding the African Grey's Mind..5

CHAPTER 2..11

A Bird of Many Words – The Art of Mimicry and Speech 11

CHAPTER 3..20

Emotional Feathers – The Deep Bond Between Parrots and Humans 20

CHAPTER 4..29

Wings of Wisdom – What Makes the African Grey So Smart? 29

CHAPTER 5..39

The Parrot's Perspective – How an African Grey Sees the World..39

CHAPTER 6..48

Feathered Storytellers – Famous African Greys in History...........48

CHAPTER 7..56

Caring for a Genius – Nutrition, Environment, and Mental Stimulation 56

CHAPTER 8...65

TRAINING AND TALKING – TEACHING WORDS, TRICKS, AND BEHAVIORS 65

CHAPTER 9...76

CHALLENGES OF A CLEVER BIRD – COMMON BEHAVIORAL ISSUES AND SOLUTIONS...76

CHAPTER 10...88

ECHOES OF THE WILD – THE AFRICAN GREY IN ITS NATURAL HABITAT.......88

CONCLUSION 99

Chapter 1

The Intelligent Companion – Understanding the African Grey's Mind

The African Grey Parrot is one of the most intelligent birds on the planet, possessing cognitive abilities comparable to those of a young child. These parrots are known for their exceptional memory, problem-solving skills, and ability to mimic human speech with remarkable accuracy. Understanding their mind is key to building a deep bond and ensuring their well-being. This chapter explores the cognitive abilities, emotional intelligence, and social behaviors that make the African Grey a truly extraordinary companion.

1. The Intelligence of the African Grey Parrot
The African Grey (Psittacus erithacus) is often considered the Einstein of the bird world. Studies have shown that these parrots possess reasoning abilities similar to those of a five-year-old child. Their problem-solving skills, ability to understand abstract

concepts, and memory retention set them apart from most other bird species.

- Reasoning and Problem-Solving: African Greys can associate words with meanings, solve puzzles, and even exhibit deductive reasoning. The famous African Grey, Alex, trained by Dr. Irene Pepperberg, could count, recognize colors, and even understand the concept of zero.
- Mimicry and Language Comprehension: Unlike simple repetition, African Greys demonstrate contextual understanding of words. They can use speech to communicate needs and preferences rather than just mimic sounds.
- Tool Use and Adaptability: In captivity, African Greys have been observed using tools to solve problems, such as using sticks to retrieve food from hard-to-reach places.

2. Emotional Intelligence in African Greys

African Greys are highly sensitive and emotionally intelligent birds. They experience a wide range of emotions, from joy and excitement to frustration and jealousy.

- Bonding and Attachment: These parrots form deep emotional bonds with their owners and can suffer from separation anxiety if left alone for long periods.
- Empathy and Mood Sensitivity: Many owners report that their African Grey seems to understand human emotions, offering comfort when they sense sadness or stress.
- The Need for Mental Stimulation: Due to their high intelligence, African Greys require constant mental challenges to stay happy. Boredom can lead to behavioral issues such as feather plucking and excessive vocalization.

3. The Social Nature of the African Grey

In the wild, African Greys live in large flocks and rely on strong social bonds for survival. This social nature translates into their behavior in captivity.

- Flock Mentality: These parrots see their human caretakers as part of their flock and expect regular interaction.
- Communication and Vocalization: African Greys use a combination of vocalizations, body language, and mimicry to communicate.

- Need for Routine: They thrive on routine and can become stressed by sudden changes in their environment or schedule.

4. Training and Cognitive Engagement

Training an African Grey is not just about teaching them tricks; it is a way to stimulate their intellect and strengthen the bond between owner and bird.

- Positive Reinforcement: Reward-based training using treats or praise helps reinforce good behavior and encourages learning.
- Interactive Games and Puzzles: Providing foraging toys and puzzle feeders can keep their mind active.
- Speech and Word Association Training: Repetition and contextual learning help African Greys understand and use words meaningfully.

5. Challenges in Understanding Their Mind

Despite their intelligence, African Greys can be challenging to care for due to their high emotional sensitivity and complex cognitive needs.

- Over-Attachment Issues: If not properly socialized, they may develop unhealthy attachments and become possessive of their owners.
- Mimicking Negative Sounds: If exposed to negative words or sounds, they may repeat them frequently, sometimes at inopportune moments.
- Mental Health and Feather Plucking: Stress, anxiety, and lack of mental stimulation can lead to destructive behaviors like feather plucking.

6. Enhancing the Mental Well-Being of Your African Grey

To ensure a healthy and happy African Grey, owners must create an enriching and intellectually stimulating environment.

- Daily Interaction and Socialization: Spending quality time talking, playing, and training with your parrot prevents loneliness and anxiety.
- Varied Diet and Foraging Activities: Encouraging natural foraging behaviors with hidden treats and food puzzles keeps their mind engaged.
- Safe and Stimulating Environment: Providing a variety of toys, swings, and safe chewing materials satisfies their need for exploration and problem-solving.

The African Grey Parrot is not just a pet; it is an intelligent, emotionally complex companion that requires patience, understanding, and constant mental engagement. By recognizing their cognitive abilities, emotional needs, and social nature, owners can build a fulfilling and lifelong bond with these extraordinary birds.

Chapter 2

A Bird of Many Words – The Art of Mimicry and Speech

The African Grey Parrot is renowned for its ability to mimic human speech with remarkable accuracy, often forming deep emotional bonds with its owners through vocal communication. But beyond simple mimicry, these birds demonstrate an understanding of language, context, and tone that sets them apart from other talking birds.

In this chapter, we will explore the science behind their vocal abilities, the role of mimicry in their natural and captive environments, techniques for training them to speak, and the deeper implications of their speech abilities.

1. The Science Behind African Grey Parrot Speech
Unlike humans, parrots do not have vocal cords. Instead, they produce sound by manipulating the syrinx, a unique vocal organ located at the base of their trachea. This allows them to create an

impressive range of sounds, from whistles and beeps to full sentences spoken in perfect human-like tones.

- The Syrinx and Its Role in Speech: The syrinx has finely tuned muscles that allow African Greys to control pitch, volume, and tone with incredible precision.
- Brain Structure and Intelligence: African Greys have a highly developed pallium, the part of the brain responsible for problem-solving, learning, and memory. This advanced neural structure contributes to their ability to process and reproduce complex sounds.
- Understanding vs. Mimicry: While many birds mimic sounds purely for social interaction, African Greys appear to understand context, recognizing when and how to use certain words appropriately.

Key Studies on African Grey Speech

One of the most famous studies on African Grey intelligence involved Alex, a parrot studied by Dr. Irene Pepperberg. Alex demonstrated the ability to:

- Identify objects, colors, and numbers.

- Understand abstract concepts like "bigger," "smaller," and "same."
- Respond to questions in a meaningful way rather than just repeating sounds.
- These findings suggest that African Greys do more than mimic—they process language on a deeper cognitive level.

2. Mimicry in the Wild vs. Captivity

African Greys develop their vocal abilities for different reasons depending on their environment.

Speech in the Wild

In their natural habitat, African Greys use vocalization for:

- Flock Communication: Different calls are used to signal danger, find food, or maintain social bonds.
- Mimicry as Camouflage: Some wild African Greys have been observed mimicking the sounds of predators or other birds to blend into their environment.
- Social Learning: Young parrots learn vocalizations by listening to and copying their elders.

Speech in Captivity

In a home setting, mimicry serves a different purpose:

- Human Interaction: African Greys see their owners as part of their flock and mimic human speech to bond with them.
- Attention-Seeking: Many birds quickly learn that certain words or phrases get a reaction, such as saying "Hello" when someone enters a room.
- Emotional Expression: Some parrots use speech to express emotions, such as saying "I love you" to a favorite person or imitating a comforting tone.

3. Training an African Grey to Speak

Teaching an African Grey to speak is a rewarding process that strengthens the bond between bird and owner. While some parrots begin speaking naturally, others require structured training.

Step 1: Creating the Right Environment

- A Calm, Quiet Space: Background noise should be minimized to help the bird focus on human speech.
- Consistent Interaction: Daily conversations and one-on-one time encourage vocalization.

- Positive Reinforcement: Rewarding speech with treats, praise, or petting reinforces learning.

Step 2: Choosing Words and Phrases
- Start with Simple Words: "Hello," "Goodbye," and the bird's name are easy starting points.
- Use Context: Saying "Good morning" when entering the room helps the bird associate words with actions.
- Repeat Clearly and Often: Repetition helps the parrot grasp pronunciation and meaning.

Step 3: Advancing to Complex Speech
Once the bird masters basic words, more complex phrases can be introduced.

- Conversational Training: Asking simple questions and waiting for responses encourages dialogue.
- Interactive Games: Teaching the bird to name objects by holding them up and saying their names strengthens word association.
- Mimicking Emotion and Tone: African Greys can learn to express emotion by mimicking tone, such as saying "Oh no!" in a worried voice.

4. The Challenges of a Talking Bird

Owning an African Grey with advanced speech abilities comes with its own set of challenges.

Unwanted or Inappropriate Speech

- Picking Up Bad Words: African Greys have a habit of mimicking phrases they hear frequently, including curse words.
- Mimicking Household Sounds: Some parrots copy doorbells, microwaves, or alarms, leading to confusion for owners.
- Repetitive Talking: A bored or attention-seeking African Grey may repeat certain words or sounds excessively.

Managing Problematic Speech

- Ignore Unwanted Words: Reacting to bad words reinforces them. Avoid responding, and the bird will eventually stop.
- Encourage Positive Speech: Rewarding desired words or phrases helps guide the parrot's vocabulary.
- Provide Mental Stimulation: Keeping the bird engaged with toys, puzzles, and training prevents excessive vocalization.

5. Understanding the Deeper Meaning Behind Parrot Speech

Many owners believe their African Grey truly "talks" to them, and science suggests there may be more to their speech than simple mimicry.

Do African Greys Understand What They Say?

- Contextual Use: Birds like Alex demonstrated an ability to use words meaningfully, indicating an understanding of context.
- Emotional Connection: Some parrots use words in response to emotions, such as saying "I miss you" when left alone.
- Predicting Actions: African Greys can learn routines and say appropriate phrases at the right time, such as "Time for bed" at night.

Can They Develop Their Own Sentences?

While parrots don't create new sentences in the way humans do, some learn to combine words in novel ways. Owners have reported birds saying unique phrases that suggest a deeper grasp of language, such as:

- "Want apple, please" when requesting food.

- "Where are you going?" when an owner leaves the room.
- "What's wrong?" when sensing someone's sadness.

This suggests that, while parrots may not form entirely new sentences, they do develop an advanced understanding of word association and emotional expression.

6. The Future of African Grey Language Studies

As research continues, scientists are uncovering more about the African Grey's linguistic abilities.

Current Research Areas
- Parrot Cognition and AI: Studies are being conducted to compare African Grey speech processing with artificial intelligence language models.
- Neural Mapping: Brain imaging technology is helping researchers understand how parrots process and store language.
- Long-Term Memory and Speech Retention: Some studies suggest African Greys can remember words and phrases for years, even if not frequently used.

What This Means for Owners

Understanding the depth of an African Grey's cognitive abilities can help owners:

- Foster deeper bonds by treating their birds as intelligent companions.
- Use language training as a way to mentally stimulate and engage their parrots.
- Respect their parrot's emotional and social needs, recognizing that speech is a significant part of their communication.

The African Grey Parrot is much more than a simple mimic—it is a highly intelligent, emotionally perceptive, and socially aware bird capable of meaningful vocal interactions. Whether engaging in playful conversation, expressing emotions, or responding to its environment, an African Grey's speech is a window into its brilliant mind.

By understanding and nurturing their linguistic abilities, owners can unlock the full potential of their feathered companion, fostering a relationship built on communication, trust, and mutual understanding.

Chapter 3

Emotional Feathers – The Deep Bond Between Parrots and Humans

Their ability to form deep bonds with their human caregivers is not just a result of their intelligence but also their emotional sensitivity. Unlike many other pets, parrots see their owners as part of their flock, relying on them for social interaction, mental stimulation, and emotional support.

This chapter explores the depth of emotional connection between African Greys and their human companions, the psychological needs of these birds, the process of bonding, and the challenges that arise when such deep bonds are not nurtured properly.

1. Understanding the Emotional Intelligence of African Grey Parrots

African Grey Parrots are often compared to young children in terms of their intelligence and emotional capacity. Studies have shown that these birds:

- Experience a Range of Emotions – They display joy, sadness, fear, jealousy, and even frustration.
- Form Deep Attachments – Once bonded, an African Grey can become deeply devoted to a specific person.
- Recognize Human Emotions – Many owners report that their parrots respond to their moods, offering comfort when they are sad or excitement when they return home.

The Science Behind Parrot Emotions
Research in avian neuroscience has found that parrots have a highly developed pallium, the part of the brain responsible for learning, problem-solving, and emotional processing. Unlike many other birds, African Greys exhibit behaviors that suggest an understanding of emotional context, not just instinctive reactions.

Dr. Irene Pepperberg's work with Alex, the famous African Grey, demonstrated that parrots can express preferences, ask for what they want, and even become frustrated when misunderstood—traits commonly associated with emotional intelligence.

2. The Process of Bonding with an African Grey
Building a bond with an African Grey is a gradual and delicate process that requires trust, patience, and consistent interaction.

The bond is not automatic; it must be cultivated through daily experiences.

Stages of Bonding
- Observation and Trust Building – When a parrot first arrives in a new home, it will observe its surroundings and the people in it before deciding whom to trust.
- Recognizing Flock Members – Once comfortable, the parrot starts seeing its human family as part of its flock and engages in social behaviors.
- Establishing Communication – Through vocalization, body language, and eye contact, the African Grey learns to communicate with its chosen human.
- Deep Emotional Connection – With time, the parrot develops an attachment similar to that of a young child with a parent, seeking comfort, affection, and companionship.

Signs of a Strong Bond
- Prefers being around you and follows you around the house.
- Mimics your voice or specific words you frequently say.
- Grooms or preens you, indicating affection.

- Reacts to your emotions and offers vocal comfort.

3. The Role of Speech and Communication in Bonding

African Greys use a combination of speech, mimicry, and body language to bond with their human caregivers.

How Parrots Communicate Emotionally
- Mimicry as Affection – A bonded African Grey will often mimic its owner's words and phrases in a way that reflects emotional connection.
- Tone Matching – Many parrots adjust their vocal tone to match their owner's emotional state, using soothing tones when their human is upset.
- Physical Gestures – Wing flaring, bowing, and beak clicking can indicate trust and affection.

Developing a Language of Love

Just as humans use words and gestures to express emotions, African Greys develop their own "language" to communicate with their owners. Some owners report their birds using comforting phrases like "I love you" or "Come here" in appropriate contexts, reinforcing the emotional depth of their bond.

4. Emotional Dependency and Separation Anxiety

Because African Greys form such strong bonds, they can suffer from emotional distress if they feel abandoned or neglected.

Signs of Separation Anxiety
- Excessive calling or screaming when the owner leaves the room.
- Feather plucking due to stress or loneliness.
- Loss of appetite or lethargy when left alone for long periods.

Preventing Emotional Distress
- Routine and Stability – Parrots thrive on consistency, so maintaining a daily schedule helps reduce stress.
- Mental Stimulation – Providing toys, interactive games, and foraging opportunities keeps their mind engaged.
- Socialization with Multiple People – Encouraging interaction with different family members prevents over-attachment to a single person.

5. Challenges of an Overly Attached Parrot

While a strong bond is a positive aspect of parrot ownership, excessive attachment can lead to behavioral issues.

Common Problems

- Possessiveness – An African Grey may become territorial over its favorite person, displaying aggression towards others.
- Jealousy – If another pet or person gets attention, the parrot might act out by screaming, biting, or interrupting conversations.
- Clinginess – Some African Greys demand constant attention and become distressed when their owner is not around.

Solutions

- Encourage Independence – Teaching a parrot to entertain itself with toys and foraging activities helps reduce clinginess.
- Balanced Attention – Giving equal interaction time to other pets and family members discourages possessiveness.
- Gradual Alone-Time Training – Leaving the bird alone for short periods and gradually increasing the duration helps it adjust to being alone without distress.

6. The Healing Power of the Parrot-Human Bond

Many parrot owners describe their African Greys as emotional support animals due to their ability to provide companionship and comfort.

Parrots as Therapy Companions
- Reducing Stress and Anxiety – The presence of a bonded parrot can have a calming effect, much like therapy animals in hospitals and nursing homes.
- Easing Loneliness – For people living alone, an African Grey can become a cherished companion.
- Encouraging Social Interaction – Owning a parrot often leads to conversations with fellow bird enthusiasts, fostering social connections.

Real-Life Stories of Emotional Healing
Many owners share heartwarming stories of their parrots sensing their emotions and responding with affection. Some African Greys have been known to say comforting phrases like "It's okay" or "Don't worry" when their owners are upset.

7. The Ethical Responsibility of Owning an Emotionally Intelligent Bird

Because African Greys are highly social and emotionally sensitive, they require significant commitment and responsibility from their owners.

Key Ethical Considerations
- Avoiding Neglect – An African Grey should never be left alone for extended periods without stimulation.
- Providing a Stable Home – Frequent rehoming or unstable environments can cause severe emotional distress.
- Recognizing Their Emotional Needs – Owners must be attentive to their parrot's emotions and respond with care and understanding.

Lifelong Commitment:
African Greys have a lifespan of 40–60 years, meaning they often outlive their owners. Ensuring a proper long-term care plan is essential to maintaining their well-being.

The bond between African Grey Parrots and their human companions is a unique and profound relationship built on trust, communication, and emotional connection. These birds are not just pets; they are lifelong companions capable of deep affection, empathy, and loyalty.

To truly appreciate and nurture the intelligence and emotional depth of an African Grey, owners must commit to providing a stable, loving, and engaging environment. In return, these remarkable parrots offer a level of companionship that few other animals can match, forming a friendship that lasts a lifetime.

Chapter 4

Wings of Wisdom – What Makes the African Grey So Smart?

The African Grey Parrot is often regarded as one of the most intelligent bird species in the world, capable of complex problem-solving, emotional understanding, and sophisticated vocal communication. Their remarkable cognitive abilities rival those of great apes and young children, making them one of the most fascinating creatures in the animal kingdom.

In this chapter, we explore the depth of the African Grey's intelligence, the scientific studies that prove their cognitive prowess, and the ways in which these birds use their intelligence in both the wild and captivity.

1. Understanding Intelligence in African Grey Parrots
Intelligence in animals is typically measured by their ability to learn, solve problems, remember information, and communicate effectively. African Greys excel in all of these areas.

Key Indicators of Intelligence
- Problem-Solving Skills – They can figure out how to open cages, unlock latches, and retrieve hidden food.
- Complex Communication – They use speech and vocal mimicry to interact with humans and other birds.
- Memory and Learning – They remember words, commands, and even people for years.
- Emotional Awareness – They react to human emotions, displaying empathy and social intelligence.
- Their intelligence goes beyond simple mimicry—they understand the context, recognize cause and effect, and even engage in logical reasoning.

2. The Science Behind Their Intelligence

The African Grey's intelligence has been a subject of scientific study for decades, with groundbreaking research revealing their cognitive capabilities.

Brain Structure and Cognitive Function

Despite their small size, African Greys have a brain-to-body ratio comparable to that of primates. Their intelligence is largely attributed to:

- Well-Developed Pallium – The pallium in birds is analogous to the cerebral cortex in mammals, responsible for reasoning and learning.
- Neural Density – African Greys have a high concentration of neurons, particularly in areas related to problem-solving and communication.
- Enhanced Memory Processing – Studies suggest they have both short-term and long-term memory retention, allowing them to recall words and events for years.

Groundbreaking Research on African Grey Intelligence

One of the most famous studies on African Greys was conducted by Dr. Irene Pepperberg, who worked with a parrot named Alex. Alex demonstrated an ability to:

- Identify and categorize objects by shape, color, and material.
- Understand numerical concepts, including the concept of zero.
- Ask for and refuse specific items based on his preferences.
- Use language meaningfully, not just mimic sounds.

Dr. Pepperberg's research proved that African Greys are capable of logical reasoning and complex thought processes, rivaling young children in their cognitive abilities.

3. Problem-Solving and Logical Thinking

African Greys demonstrate remarkable problem-solving abilities, using logic and experimentation to navigate challenges.

Examples of Problem-Solving in African Greys

- Puzzle Solving – They can manipulate puzzle toys to access food rewards.
- Tool Use – Some African Greys have been observed using objects as tools to retrieve treats.
- Escape Tactics – Many parrots figure out how to open cage doors and undo locks.
- Logical Deduction – Studies show they can make inferences, choosing the correct solution without trial and error.

These problem-solving abilities suggest advanced reasoning skills, not just instinctive behaviors.

4. Memory and Learning Abilities

African Greys possess an exceptional memory, allowing them to recall words, people, and experiences over long periods.

Short-Term vs. Long-Term Memory
- Short-Term Memory – Helps them quickly learn new words and solve puzzles.
- Long-Term Memory – Allows them to remember learned vocabulary and familiar people, even after years of separation.

Learning Through Imitation and Repetition
African Greys learn through observation and repetition. They:

- Copy human speech patterns and voice inflections.
- Recognize and recall phrases associated with specific actions or emotions.
- Learn by watching other birds or humans perform tasks.

This ability to observe and apply knowledge is a hallmark of advanced intelligence.

5. Social and Emotional Intelligence

One of the most remarkable aspects of African Grey intelligence is their emotional depth and ability to form strong social bonds.

- **How They Exhibit Emotional Intelligence**
- Recognizing Human Emotions – Many owners report that their parrots comfort them when they are sad or anxious.
- Jealousy and Possessiveness – They can show jealousy if their favorite person pays attention to another pet or person.
- Empathy and Social Bonds – They form deep emotional connections with their caregivers, much like dogs and other highly intelligent animals.

African Greys and Emotional Responses

Studies show that African Greys can:

- React differently to familiar vs. unfamiliar people.
- Exhibit behaviors that indicate affection, fear, or frustration.
- Modify their vocal tone based on the emotional state of their owner.

Their social intelligence makes them highly interactive and emotionally engaging companions.

6. Speech and Communication Abilities

African Greys are famous for their speech abilities, but their talent goes beyond simple mimicry.

How They Use Language
- Contextual Speech – Many African Greys use words in meaningful ways, such as greeting their owners when they enter a room.
- Question and Response – Some parrots can answer simple questions correctly, showing comprehension.
- Phrase Customization – Some African Greys create new phrases by combining learned words.
- Differences Between Mimicry and Understanding
- Mimicry – Simply repeating sounds without understanding.
- Contextual Understanding – Using words appropriately, such as saying "Want apple" when hungry.

African Greys are among the few animals that can use words intentionally, rather than just imitate sounds.

7. Adaptability and Intelligence in the Wild

In their natural habitat, African Greys use their intelligence for survival, communication, and problem-solving.

How They Use Intelligence in the Wild
- Complex Vocalizations – They communicate with flock members using distinct calls.
- Memory for Food Sources – They remember the locations of fruiting trees and water sources.
- Predator Evasion – They use vocal warnings and collective defense strategies against predators.
- Differences Between Wild and Captive Intelligence
- Wild African Greys use intelligence for navigation, survival, and social interaction.
- Captive African Greys use intelligence for communication with humans, puzzle-solving, and emotional bonding.

Their adaptability in both environments highlights their exceptional cognitive abilities.

8. The Future of Intelligence Studies in African Greys

Scientists continue to study African Grey intelligence to understand animal cognition and communication.

Current Research Areas
- Artificial Intelligence Comparisons – Studying how parrots process language compared to AI models.
- Neural Imaging – Mapping brain activity to understand memory and decision-making.
- Emotional Intelligence Studies – Examining how parrots perceive and respond to human emotions.

Implications for the Future
- Better Understanding of Animal Cognition – African Greys challenge our understanding of non-human intelligence.
- Ethical Considerations – Their intelligence raises ethical concerns about keeping them in captivity.
- Enhanced Training Methods – Research can improve how we train and interact with parrots.

The African Grey Parrot's intelligence is nothing short of extraordinary. From problem-solving and speech abilities to emotional intelligence and memory, they possess cognitive skills that rival those of primates and young children.

Understanding and nurturing their intelligence requires dedication, patience, and respect for their emotional and mental needs. In return, these brilliant birds offer companionship, conversation, and a lifelong bond that few other animals can provide.

Chapter 5

The Parrot's Perspective – How an African Grey Sees the World

Their vision, cognition, emotions, and sensory perceptions shape their unique way of experiencing life. Understanding how an African Grey sees the world can help owners develop stronger bonds with their birds, provide enriching environments, and foster deeper communication.

This chapter explores the African Grey's world through its physical senses, cognitive processing, emotions, social interactions, and environmental perception.

1. Vision – Seeing the World with Parrot Eyes
Birds, including African Greys, have superior vision compared to humans, allowing them to perceive colors and movement in ways we cannot.

How an African Grey's Vision Differs from Humans

- Wide Field of View – African Greys have eyes positioned on the sides of their heads, giving them a nearly 300-degree field of vision.
- Monocular and Binocular Vision – They can use one eye independently or both together for depth perception.Ultraviolet (UV) Vision – Unlike humans, African Greys can see ultraviolet light, which helps them:

1. Identify ripe fruits.
2. Recognize flock members.
3. Detect subtle changes in feathers that indicate health or mood.

How Their Vision Affects Their Behavior
- Quick Response to Movement – African Greys notice even the smallest movements, which is why they can be startled easily.
- Recognizing Their Owners – They don't just recognize faces; they also distinguish people based on clothing colors and UV light reflections.
- Fear of Shadows and Sudden Light Changes – A sudden change in lighting can confuse or frighten them, as their eyes quickly adjust to different intensities.

African Greys see a world rich in colors, textures, and movements, making their visual experience much more dynamic than ours.

2. Cognitive Perception – Thinking Like an African Grey

Beyond physical vision, African Greys have remarkable cognitive abilities, allowing them to interpret their world logically and emotionally.

How African Greys Process Information
- Pattern Recognition – They learn routines quickly and expect consistency in their environment.
- Object Permanence – Unlike some animals, African Greys understand that objects still exist even when hidden, which is why they enjoy hide-and-seek games.
- Anticipation and Prediction – They can predict outcomes based on past experiences, such as expecting food when they see a treat container.

Understanding Time and Sequences
- Daily Routine Awareness – They anticipate feeding times, playtime, and when their owners will leave or return home.

- Memory Retention – African Greys remember people, objects, and past experiences for years.
- Future Planning – They show decision-making skills when selecting tools or choosing between different rewards.

African Greys don't just react to their environment; they analyze it, predict outcomes, and form logical conclusions.

3. Emotional Experience – Feeling the World Through a Parrot's Heart

African Greys are highly emotional creatures, capable of experiencing complex feelings similar to those of young children.

How They Express Emotions
- Happiness – Purring, wing-flapping, beak grinding, and relaxed feathers.
- Fear – Wide eyes, flared wings, crouching, and freezing in place.
- Jealousy – Vocal protests, interrupting conversations, or pushing other pets away.
- Loneliness – Excessive calling, feather plucking, and reduced activity.

Understanding Their Emotional Sensitivity
- They Read Human Emotions – African Greys often mirror their owner's mood and can become stressed if their human is anxious or sad.
- They Form Strong Bonds – They see their owner as a flock member, sometimes displaying separation anxiety when left alone.
- They Hold Grudges and Forgive – If they feel betrayed (e.g., forced into a cage), they may avoid the person until trust is rebuilt.

Emotions play a huge role in how an African Grey interprets its world, making them deeply social and sensitive companions.

4. Communication and Social Perception
African Greys communicate not just through words but also through body language, tone, and vocal cues.

How They Understand Human Communication
- Tone Matters More Than Words – They respond more to the emotion behind a voice rather than the words themselves.

- Facial Expressions and Gestures – They notice human facial expressions and match their reactions accordingly.
- Conversational Awareness – Many African Greys participate in conversations by inserting words or sounds at the right moments.

How They Communicate with Other Birds
- Mimicking Calls – In the wild, they copy the vocalizations of their flock members to fit in.
- Understanding Hierarchies – They recognize social structures within groups, both among birds and in human families.
- Body Language – Head bobbing, eye pinning, and feather positioning all convey different messages.

To an African Grey, communication is a two-way interaction, filled with emotions, observations, and intelligent responses.

5. Environmental Awareness – Interacting with the World Around Them
African Greys are incredibly observant and highly sensitive to their surroundings.

How They Interpret Their Environment
- Height Equals Safety – They feel more secure when perched at a high vantage point.
- New Objects Can Be Scary – Sudden changes, such as a new toy or rearranged furniture, might cause initial fear.
- They Learn Through Exploration – They use their beak to taste and touch objects, helping them understand new things.

How They React to Their Surroundings
- Sound Sensitivity – They can hear subtle sounds long before humans notice them. Sudden noises can startle them.
- Changes in Routine Can Be Stressful – Moving homes, changing cages, or introducing new pets can disrupt their sense of security.
- Recognizing Danger – African Greys rely on their sharp instincts to assess threats, sometimes reacting strongly to unfamiliar people or animals.

Their world is deeply shaped by routine, observation, and interaction, making them incredibly aware of every detail in their environment.

6. The Role of Play and Learning in Their Perspective

For an African Grey, play is learning, and every interaction contributes to their understanding of the world.

Why Play is Essential

- Mental Stimulation – Puzzle toys help them engage their problem-solving skills.
- Social Bonding – Playing with their owner strengthens trust and attachment.
- Exploration – They investigate objects by chewing, tapping, and tossing them.

Favorite Types of Play

- Interactive Talking Games – They enjoy repeating words and testing new sounds.
- Puzzles and Foraging – Hiding treats inside toys helps stimulate their natural curiosity.
- Mimicry-Based Play – Copying sounds, music, or laughter is a form of entertainment for them.

By playing and experimenting, African Greys constantly refine their understanding of their world.

An African Grey's perception of the world is vivid, emotional, and highly intelligent. They see ultraviolet colors, understand complex social cues, process emotions deeply, and learn through both observation and experience.

Understanding their unique perspective helps owners provide a more enriching and respectful environment, allowing for a deeper and more meaningful bond.

To truly connect with an African Grey, one must see the world through their eyes, understanding their fears, joys, and intelligence. By doing so, we open the door to a remarkable friendship that is as rewarding as it is enlightening.

Chapter 6

Feathered Storytellers – Famous African Greys in History

Throughout history, some African Greys have gained fame for their exceptional talents, intelligence, and interactions with humans. From groundbreaking scientific research to beloved celebrity pets, these birds have proven time and again that they are far more than just mimics—they are storytellers, thinkers, and even problem solvers.

In this chapter, we will explore some of the most famous African Greys in history, their contributions to science and culture, and the lessons we can learn from their remarkable lives.

1. The Most Famous African Grey – Alex
No discussion of famous African Greys would be complete without mentioning Alex, the legendary parrot who changed the way we understand avian intelligence.

The Groundbreaking Work of Dr. Irene Pepperberg

Alex was the subject of a 30-year research project led by Dr. Irene Pepperberg, a scientist who sought to understand how birds think, communicate, and learn. Through her work with Alex, she demonstrated that African Greys:

- Could understand and use human language meaningfully, not just mimic sounds.
- Had the ability to count and even understood the concept of zero.
- Could categorize objects by shape, color, and material.
- Used logical reasoning to solve problems.

Alex's Amazing Abilities:
- Vocabulary of over 100 words – Alex could name objects, ask for things, and even express his preferences.
- Understanding of numbers – He could count up to six and understood the difference between "more" and "less."
- Emotional intelligence – Alex developed strong social bonds and even asked existential questions like "What color am I?"

The Heartbreaking Goodbye:

- Alex's last words to Dr. Pepperberg before he passed away in 2007 were:
- "You are good. I love you. See you tomorrow."

His legacy continues to shape the way scientists and bird lovers understand African Greys.

2. Einstein – The Celebrity Parrot

Another famous African Grey, Einstein, became a worldwide sensation for his incredible talking ability and sense of humor.

Einstein's Rise to Fame
- He gained popularity through performances at the Knoxville Zoo in Tennessee.
- Featured on TV shows like The Oprah Winfrey Show and Animal Planet.
- Became a viral sensation with his ability to mimic over 200 words and sounds.

Einstein's Unique Talents:
- Impersonations – He could mimic other animals, including horses, dogs, and even a spaceship sound.

- Playful Personality – He often "joked" by responding with unexpected but humorous phrases.
- Command of Language – While not scientifically studied like Alex, Einstein demonstrated an uncanny ability to use words in appropriate contexts.

Einstein proved that African Greys not only learn words but also use them in creative and entertaining ways.

3. N'kisi – The Parrot with a Sense of Humor

N'kisi is an African Grey known for his impressive vocabulary and advanced linguistic abilities.

What Made N'kisi Special?
- Vocabulary of over 1,000 words – One of the largest recorded for an African Grey.
- Use of Grammar and Sentence Structure – Unlike most parrots, he could form full sentences and use words in proper contexts.
- Sense of Humor and Sarcasm – He often made witty remarks, displaying an understanding of humor.

Examples of His Intelligence:

- When seeing a picture of Jane Goodall with a chimpanzee, N'kisi remarked: "Got a chimp?"
- He used past and future tense, indicating an understanding of time.
- When left alone, he sometimes spoke to himself, demonstrating internal thought processes.

N'kisi's abilities raised new questions about how parrots perceive language and their ability to think independently.

4. Prudle – The Champion Talker

Prudle was an African Grey who held the Guinness World Record for the Most Talking Words for many years.

Prudle's Notable Achievements:

Vocabulary of over 800 words.

- Was found in the jungle of Uganda and later became a famous pet in England.
- Recognized for his clear speech and ability to learn new words quickly.

Prudle's story demonstrated that even wild African Greys could develop extraordinary communication skills in captivity.

5. Mishka – The YouTube Star

Mishka gained internet fame as one of the first African Greys to become a social media sensation.

Mishka's Special Abilities:
- Known for saying "I love you" in a heartfelt tone.
- Learned to use words in contextually appropriate ways.
- Became a viral star with millions of views on YouTube.

Mishka's story highlights the bond between African Greys and their owners in the digital age.

6. African Greys in History and Culture

Parrots in Ancient Egypt:
- African Greys were kept as pets by Egyptian nobles.
- Hieroglyphs suggest that parrots were valued for their beauty and intelligence.

Parrots in Royalty:

- King Henry VIII had an African Grey that entertained guests with speech.
- Queen Victoria was also known to keep exotic birds, including African Greys.

Parrots in Literature and Media:
- Long John Silver's parrot in "Treasure Island" is based on real-life talking parrots.
- African Greys have appeared in countless books, films, and cartoons, symbolizing wisdom and wit.

7. What These Famous Parrots Teach Us

These legendary African Greys provide us with important lessons:

1. Parrots Are Highly Intelligent

They are capable of problem-solving, emotional connections, and even creative thinking.

2. They Need Mental Stimulation

Without engagement, they can become bored and develop behavioral issues.

3. They Form Deep Emotional Bonds

Many of these famous parrots were deeply attached to their owners, showing empathy and loyalty.

4. They Have a Unique View of the World
Their ability to mimic speech and understand context offers insight into their cognitive abilities.

5. They Deserve Ethical Treatment
Their intelligence raises ethical concerns about how they are kept and treated in captivity.

African Greys have long been admired for their intelligence, speech abilities, and emotional depth. From the groundbreaking research of Alex to the celebrity antics of Einstein and Mishka, these birds continue to astonish and inspire.

Understanding their cognitive abilities not only deepens our appreciation for these magnificent creatures but also challenges our assumptions about animal intelligence and communication.

Perhaps, as we learn more from these feathered storytellers, we will also discover new ways to communicate with and respect the natural world.

Chapter 7

Caring for a Genius – Nutrition, Environment, and Mental Stimulation

African Grey parrots are often considered the Einsteins of the bird world. With their high intelligence, emotional depth, and complex social needs, they require more than just food and a cage to thrive. Proper care for an African Grey involves balanced nutrition, a stimulating environment, and continuous mental engagement. Without these, they can suffer from nutritional deficiencies, boredom, stress, and behavioral problems like feather plucking or aggression.

This chapter explores the essential aspects of caring for an African Grey: their dietary needs, ideal habitat, mental stimulation, and emotional well-being.

1. Nutrition – Fueling the Mind of a Genius
A balanced diet is crucial for African Greys. Since they are prone to calcium and vitamin A deficiencies, an improper diet can lead

to weakened bones, poor feather health, and immune system issues.

A Well-Balanced Diet for African Greys

An optimal diet consists of:

- Pellets (50-60%) – High-quality, vet-approved pellets ensure they get essential vitamins and minerals.
- Fresh Vegetables (20-25%) – Dark leafy greens, carrots, bell peppers, and sweet potatoes provide vitamin A and antioxidants.
- Fresh Fruits (10-15%) – Apples, bananas, berries, and papayas add natural sugars and fiber but should be fed in moderation.
- Healthy Grains & Legumes (5-10%) – Quinoa, brown rice, lentils, and chickpeas offer proteins and complex carbohydrates.
- Nuts & Seeds (Treats Only) – Walnuts, almonds, and sunflower seeds are rich in fats but should be given sparingly.

Foods to Avoid
- Avocado – Highly toxic to birds.

- Chocolate & Caffeine – Can cause heart issues and seizures.
- Onions & Garlic – Can damage red blood cells.
- Alcohol & Sugary Foods – Harmful to metabolism and digestion.
- Salty & Processed Foods – Can cause dehydration and kidney issues.

Importance of Calcium & Vitamin A:
- Calcium Deficiency Risks – African Greys are prone to hypocalcemia, leading to weak bones, seizures, and tremors. Provide cuttlebones, calcium supplements, and leafy greens.
- Vitamin A for Immune Health – Helps with feather growth, eye health, and disease resistance. Carrots, squash, and red bell peppers are excellent sources.

A well-balanced diet ensures longevity, strong immunity, and mental sharpness for these intelligent birds.

2. Environment – Creating a Safe and Enriching Home

The right environment plays a crucial role in an African Grey's happiness, safety, and intellectual growth. Their enclosure should mimic the complexity of their natural habitat while offering security and stimulation.

The Ideal Cage Setup:
- Size Matters – The bigger, the better. A minimum cage size is 36" x 24" x 48", but a larger space is always preferable.
- Bar Spacing – ¾ to 1 inch spacing prevents injury or escape attempts.
- Multiple Perches – Varying textures and diameters help strengthen foot muscles and prevent arthritis.
- Foraging and Feeding Stations – Encourages natural food-hunting behaviors to prevent boredom.
- Toys and Play Areas – Keeps them mentally engaged (more on this in the stimulation section).

Environmental Conditions:
- Temperature – 65-80°F is ideal; avoid extreme heat or cold.
- Humidity Levels – African Greys thrive in 50-70% humidity. Dry environments can cause feather issues and respiratory problems.

Natural Light and Sleep Schedule :

- They need 10-12 hours of sleep in a quiet, dark area.
- Exposure to UV light (natural or artificial) helps with vitamin D production and calcium absorption.

Safe Spaces and Emotional Security:
African Greys are sensitive and cautious. They need a consistent, secure environment to feel at ease.

- Avoid sudden changes in their surroundings.
- Provide a safe hiding spot (a small hut or perch away from main activity).
- Introduce new objects gradually to prevent stress or fear-based reactions.

A structured, comfortable, and engaging environment is key to maintaining a happy, well-adjusted African Grey.

3. Mental Stimulation – Keeping a Genius Engaged
An African Grey's biggest need—beyond food and shelter—is mental engagement. Without stimulation, they can become depressed, destructive, or aggressive.

Why Mental Stimulation is Critical:

- Prevents Boredom & Depression – African Greys need constant challenges to stay mentally sharp.
- Encourages Problem-Solving – Engaging their brains through puzzles and foraging activities mimics their natural behaviors.
- Strengthens the Bond with Owners – Training sessions and social interaction build trust and companionship.

Types of Mental Stimulation

1. Interactive Toys & Puzzles
   - Foraging Toys – Hide treats inside puzzle feeders to encourage problem-solving.
   - Chewable Toys – Wooden toys, shreddable paper, and ropes satisfy their need to chew and explore.
   - Mechanical Toys – Some birds enjoy turning gears or pressing buttons to activate sounds or get treats.

2. Training & Learning Activities
   - Speech Training – African Greys are excellent mimics. Repeating words and phrases daily strengthens their cognitive skills.

- Trick Training – Teaching them to wave, fetch, or spin stimulates learning and deepens owner-bird interaction.
- Target Training – Encourages them to follow a target (a stick or hand) to build focus and trust.

3. Social Interaction & Emotional Stimulation

African Greys are highly social and crave companionship and conversation.

- Daily Interaction (at least 2-4 hours) – Without enough attention, they can develop separation anxiety.
- Encourage Conversations – They thrive on back-and-forth vocal exchanges.
- Play Music or Audiobooks – Helps keep them entertained when alone.
- Rotate Toys Weekly – Prevents boredom by offering new challenges regularly.

Without mental engagement, an African Grey can lose interest in food, become withdrawn, or start destructive behaviors like feather plucking.

4. Emotional Well-Being – The Social & Psychological Needs of an African Grey

An African Grey's intelligence also makes them emotionally complex. They experience a range of emotions, from happiness and excitement to jealousy and depression.

Recognizing Their Emotional State:
- Happy & Engaged – Talking, playing, purring, beak grinding.
- Anxious or Scared – Fluffed-up feathers, hiding, silence.
- Frustrated or Bored – Screaming, biting, repetitive pacing.
- Depressed or Lonely – Feather plucking, loss of appetite, low energy.

Building a Strong Bond:
- Respect Their Space – Some Greys are more independent than others; don't force interaction.
- Create Positive Associations – Use treats and praise to reinforce good behavior.
- Avoid Punishment – Negative reinforcement can lead to trust issues and fear.

Separation Anxiety & Solutions:

African Greys bond deeply with their owners and may struggle with being left alone.

- Leave a Radio or TV On – Background noise can reduce loneliness.
- Provide a Safe Companion – If possible, having another bird (even a different species) can offer comfort.
- Practice Short Absences – Train them to handle alone time gradually.

Emotional health is just as important as physical health, and a happy African Grey is an engaged, loving, and well-adjusted companion.

Caring for an African Grey goes beyond food and shelter—it requires mental challenges, emotional security, and social interaction. As some of the most intelligent creatures on Earth, they thrive in environments that stimulate their minds and nurture their emotional needs.

By understanding their nutritional needs, creating a stimulating home, and providing daily engagement, owners can ensure that these remarkable birds live long, happy, and fulfilling lives.

Chapter 8

Training and Talking – Teaching Words, Tricks, and Behaviors

Training an African Grey parrot is a rewarding and engaging process that can significantly strengthen the bond between the bird and its owner. These birds are intelligent, social, and capable of learning a wide range of words, tricks, and behaviors. They thrive in environments where they are mentally challenged and stimulated, and one of the best ways to achieve this is through training. Whether you want to teach your African Grey to mimic human speech, perform impressive tricks, or behave appropriately, understanding the principles of training is essential.

This chapter delves into the art of training and talking with an African Grey, exploring effective techniques for teaching words, tricks, and positive behaviors.

1. The Science of Parrot Training

Before diving into specific techniques, it's essential to understand why African Greys can be trained so successfully. Their intelligence, combined with their social nature, makes them excellent learners. However, like any intelligent animal, they require the right approach for training to be effective.

The Importance of Positive Reinforcement

Positive reinforcement is the most effective training method for African Greys. This technique involves rewarding the bird for desired behaviors, which encourages them to repeat those actions. Rewards can be in the form of:

- Treats – Small, healthy snacks or favorite foods.
- Praise – Verbal encouragement or a gentle "good bird" spoken in an enthusiastic tone.
- Toys – A new or favorite toy that reinforces the activity.

The idea behind positive reinforcement is that the bird learns that performing a certain behavior results in a pleasant outcome, which motivates them to repeat it. Conversely, negative reinforcement (punishing undesirable behavior) should be avoided, as it can create stress, fear, and distrust, ultimately hindering the training process.

The Role of Consistency and Repetition

African Greys learn best when training sessions are short, consistent, and repetitive. Regular training is vital to ensuring that the bird retains what it learns and continues to build upon it. Training sessions should last no longer than 10-15 minutes to keep the bird engaged without overwhelming it. Consistency is equally important; the same words, cues, and actions should be used repeatedly to reinforce learning.

2. Teaching Words – The Gift of Speech

One of the most fascinating aspects of African Grey parrots is their ability to mimic human speech. With the right approach, they can learn a wide variety of words and phrases, often using them appropriately in context. While some birds may never develop a large vocabulary, many African Greys can learn 100+ words and even use them to communicate their desires or emotions.

1. Start with Simple Words and Phrases

When teaching an African Grey to speak, begin with simple words or short phrases that have clear meanings. Words like "hello," "goodbye," or "want a treat" are ideal starting points.

- Choose words with distinct sounds – African Greys are better at picking up words that are easily distinguishable from one another.
- Use words in context – For instance, greet your bird with "hello" when entering the room, or say "want a treat" when offering food. This will help the bird associate the word with the action.
- Use repetition – Repeating words or phrases consistently will help your bird learn them faster.

2. Use Associative Learning

African Greys are keenly aware of their environment and can associate words with actions. For example, if you consistently say "step up" while encouraging your bird to step onto your finger, the bird will start to understand that the phrase means "come onto my hand." This method relies on associative learning, where the bird links the spoken word with a specific action or event.

- Use visual cues – Pair words with corresponding visual gestures. For example, say "step up" while extending your hand to encourage the bird to step on it.
- Reinforce immediately – Once the bird performs the correct action, immediately reward it with a treat or

praise. This reinforces the connection between the word and the action.

3. Expand the Vocabulary Gradually

Once your bird has mastered a few basic words, you can start expanding its vocabulary. Begin by adding new words or phrases that relate to its daily activities. For example, you might teach the bird to say "good morning" in the morning or "thank you" when receiving a treat.

- Use words that are relevant to its environment – Words related to feeding, playtime, or affection can be learned more easily.
- Keep the training sessions short – The bird's attention span is limited, so it's better to have multiple short training sessions throughout the day rather than one long one.

Remember, patience is key when training an African Grey to talk. Some birds will learn faster than others, and it's important not to rush the process.

3. Teaching Tricks – From Simple Moves to Complex Performances

In addition to teaching words, many African Grey owners enjoy teaching their birds various tricks. These tricks not only provide mental stimulation but also allow the bird to showcase its intelligence in an interactive and engaging way.

1. Start with Basic Tricks

The simplest tricks are often the best starting point. These include basic movements or behaviors that the bird can learn easily.

Step Up:

One of the first tricks you can teach an African Grey is to step onto your hand or finger. It is an essential trick that forms the foundation for other training.

- Start by holding your hand near the bird's chest.
- Say the command "step up" in a clear, enthusiastic voice.
- Gently guide the bird onto your finger.
- Reward immediately with praise or a treat when the bird steps up.

Wave:

Teaching your African Grey to wave is another simple but impressive trick.

- Hold a treat in your hand and place it in front of the bird's beak.
- Say "wave" while gently moving the bird's foot up and down.
- Reward the bird with a treat after the wave motion.

2. Building on Basic Tricks

Once your bird has mastered basic tricks, you can move on to more advanced behaviors. Some fun tricks to try include:

Spin:

Teaching your African Grey to spin can be a fun and relatively simple trick.

- Hold a treat in front of the bird's beak and guide it to spin in a circle.
- Use the command "spin" and gently help the bird complete the motion.
- Reward the bird for completing the spin.

Fetch:

Fetching objects can be an exciting and mentally stimulating trick.

- Use a small, soft object that your bird can easily grasp in its beak.
- Throw the object a short distance and encourage the bird to bring it back to you.
- Reward the bird for retrieving the object.

3. Advanced Trick Training

Once the basics are covered, you can teach more complex tricks, such as:

- Rolling Over – Teach the bird to lie on its back and roll over when commanded.
- Dancing – Encourage the bird to "dance" by moving its body or wings in response to music or verbal cues.
- Open Cage Door – With consistent training, some African Greys can learn to open a cage door with a lever or handle.

These tricks require time, patience, and consistent practice but are a testament to the incredible intelligence of African Grey parrots.

4. Addressing Behavioral Issues – Training for Good Behavior

Behavioral issues are common in African Greys, especially when they are not mentally stimulated or socialized correctly. Luckily, these issues can often be corrected with proper training techniques.

1. Preventing and Managing Biting

Biting is a natural behavior for many birds, but it can be problematic, especially when the bird is frightened or angry.

- Never punish the bird for biting, as this can cause fear and mistrust.
- Use the "beak" command – When the bird tries to bite, say "beak" in a firm but calm voice, which teaches them to relax their beak.
- Provide enough mental stimulation – A bored bird is more likely to bite. Keep them occupied with toys, foraging activities, and regular interaction.

2. Reducing Screaming

Excessive screaming is another common issue among African Greys. It often occurs when the bird is seeking attention or when it's bored or anxious.

- Provide consistent interaction and training throughout the day to keep the bird from feeling neglected.
- Ignore the bird when it screams for attention and only give attention when it is calm.
- Reward quiet behavior with praise and treats.

3. Overcoming Feather Plucking

Feather plucking can be a sign of stress, boredom, or a lack of stimulation. If your bird starts plucking, it's crucial to identify the root cause.

- Increase mental stimulation through training, toys, and interaction.
- Create a calm, stress-free environment with minimal loud noises or sudden changes.
- Consult an avian vet if the behavior persists, as there could be a medical issue involved.

5. Communication Beyond Words – Understanding Your African Grey's Needs

While African Greys are exceptional mimics, they also communicate through body language and sounds. It's important to understand these forms of communication as well.

Body Language and Vocalizations:
- Fluffed Feathers – The bird may be cold, scared, or excited.
- Tail Fanning – A sign of aggression or excitement.
- Beak Grinding – A sign of contentment and relaxation.
- Chatter and Whistles – Signs of happiness and social interaction.

Being attuned to these behaviors helps you understand your bird's emotional state and needs.

Training an African Grey parrot is a rewarding and enriching experience that not only improves behavior but also deepens the bond between the bird and its owner. Whether you're teaching words, tricks, or managing behaviors, positive reinforcement, consistency, and patience are key. African Greys are capable of learning complex behaviors and can provide years of entertainment and companionship if nurtured with love, respect, and the right training techniques.

Chapter 9

Challenges of a Clever Bird – Common Behavioral Issues and Solutions

African Grey parrots are widely known for their exceptional intelligence, emotional sensitivity, and strong communication skills. While these traits make them outstanding companions, they also present a unique set of challenges for their owners. As one of the most intelligent species of parrots, African Greys are more likely to experience behavioral problems, especially when their intellectual, emotional, and social needs are not met.

This chapter focuses on common behavioral issues faced by African Grey owners and explores effective solutions to address them. It covers a range of challenges, from boredom-induced behaviors to more serious issues such as feather plucking, aggression, and separation anxiety. By understanding the root causes of these problems and implementing the right strategies, you can ensure a happy, healthy relationship with your African Grey.

1. Boredom and Destructive Behavior

As intelligent and active birds, African Greys are naturally inquisitive and thrive in environments that offer mental stimulation. When deprived of this, they often resort to destructive behaviors, such as chewing on furniture, biting on cages, or plucking their feathers. Boredom is one of the most common reasons for unwanted behavior in African Greys.

Why Boredom Leads to Destructive Behavior

Boredom is a significant problem for African Greys because of their high cognitive capacity. These birds have an inherent need for mental challenges that keep them engaged and stimulated. Without sufficient mental and physical stimulation, African Greys will often find other ways to release their energy, which can lead to feather plucking, excessive screaming, or damage to furniture and other household items.

Solutions for Boredom-Induced Destructive Behavior:

To prevent and manage boredom-related behaviors, it's essential to keep your African Grey's environment engaging and stimulating.

Toys and Puzzle Feeders: Provide a variety of interactive toys and puzzle feeders that challenge the bird's problem-solving abilities. Toys that involve foraging, hiding treats, or manipulating objects can keep your bird entertained for hours.

Daily Interaction and Training: Set aside time each day for training sessions, play, and social interaction. Keep training sessions short and frequent—10 to 15 minutes at a time is ideal. Teaching new tricks or words provides mental stimulation and helps to channel the bird's energy in a productive way.

Rotate Toys Regularly: African Greys get bored with toys quickly. Rotate the toys and objects available to them, so they always have something "new" to explore.

Foraging Opportunities: African Greys are natural foragers, and offering them opportunities to search for food in different locations around their cage or home can provide both mental stimulation and the opportunity to engage in natural behaviors.

Enrich Their Environment: Add variety to their habitat by providing perches at different heights, mirrors, or non-toxic branches for chewing. These additions not only keep them busy but also create a more enriched, natural environment.

By addressing the root cause of destructive behaviors—boredom—you can keep your African Grey engaged, which helps mitigate damage to furniture, self-harm, and other destructive actions.

2. Feather Plucking – Understanding and Addressing the Issue

Feather plucking is one of the most concerning behavioral issues faced by African Grey parrots. It involves the bird pulling out its own feathers, which can lead to bald spots and, in severe cases, permanent damage to the feathers. This behavior is often an indication of stress, anxiety, or a deeper physical problem.

Causes of Feather Plucking

There are several potential causes of feather plucking in African Greys, including:

Boredom: As discussed earlier, a lack of mental stimulation can lead to feather plucking. When African Greys don't have enough to do, they may resort to this destructive behavior as a form of self-soothing or distraction.

Separation Anxiety: African Greys are highly social birds that form deep bonds with their owners. When left alone for long periods, they may develop separation anxiety, which can manifest in feather plucking or destructive behaviors.

Health Issues: Underlying medical problems, such as nutritional deficiencies (e.g., vitamin A or calcium), skin infections, or hormonal imbalances, can cause a bird to pluck its feathers. It's crucial to consult with an avian vet to rule out any medical issues before assuming the problem is behavioral.

Stress: External stressors, such as loud noises, unpredictable routines, or changes in the home environment, can trigger feather plucking in African Greys. These birds are sensitive to their surroundings, and any perceived threat can cause emotional distress.

Solutions to Address Feather Plucking

If your African Grey is feather plucking, it's important to first identify the underlying cause. Once the cause is determined, you can implement the appropriate solutions.

Provide More Enrichment: Ensure that your African Grey has a wide range of toys and interactive activities to keep its mind engaged. As a highly intelligent bird, mental stimulation is essential to reducing stress and boredom.

Establish a Routine: African Greys feel most comfortable in a stable environment with a consistent routine. Ensure that feeding times, playtimes, and interactions are scheduled regularly.

Reduce Stress: Minimize loud noises, sudden movements, or unfamiliar people entering the bird's space. Creating a quiet, calm environment will help your bird feel more secure.

Consult a Vet: If you suspect that the feather plucking is due to a health issue, visit an avian vet for a thorough examination. Medical issues like skin infections, parasites, or nutritional deficiencies need to be addressed for the behavior to stop.

Behavioral Modification: In some cases, you can use positive reinforcement to help curb feather plucking. When the bird refrains from plucking, reward it with treats or praise. If the plucking occurs during a stressful situation, try to redirect the bird's attention with a toy or a command.

Feather plucking is a serious issue that requires a combination of medical intervention, environmental enrichment, and behavioral modification. By addressing the root cause, you can help your bird break the cycle of plucking and regain its feather health.

3. Aggression – Dealing with Aggressive Behaviors

While African Greys are generally known for their sweet and affectionate nature, they can exhibit aggressive behaviors, especially when they feel threatened, insecure, or overstimulated. Aggression can take the form of biting, lunging, or screaming.

Causes of Aggression in African Greys

Several factors contribute to aggressive behavior in African Greys:

Fear and Insecurity: If an African Grey feels cornered or threatened, it may lash out in defense. This could be due to new environments, strangers, or other pets that intimidate the bird.

Overstimulation: African Greys can become irritated or frustrated if they are handled too much or subjected to too much noise. Overstimulation can cause them to act out in an aggressive manner.

Hormonal Changes: During breeding season, some African Greys become more territorial and may show signs of aggression toward their owners or other pets.

Poor Socialization: Birds that have not been socialized properly in their early life may develop fear-based aggression toward people or other animals.

Solutions for Aggressive Behavior

Addressing aggression in African Greys requires patience, consistency, and a careful understanding of the bird's triggers. Here are some solutions to mitigate aggression:

Avoid Physical Punishment: Never resort to punishment or physical correction for aggressive behavior. Punishing an African Grey can increase fear and anxiety, exacerbating the aggression.

Understand the Triggers: Pay close attention to the situations that trigger aggression. Does it occur when the bird is tired, hungry, or overstimulated? Identifying these triggers can help you manage the behavior and reduce its occurrence.

Use Positive Reinforcement: Reward good behavior with treats, praise, and toys. If the bird exhibits calm behavior instead of aggression, reinforce it with a reward. This helps the bird learn that calmness is more rewarding than aggression.

Provide Safe Spaces: Sometimes, an African Grey may become aggressive if it feels cornered or threatened. Providing a safe retreat (like a high perch or a separate space) where the bird can go when it feels overwhelmed can help prevent aggression.

Training and Socialization: Work on socializing your African Grey with different people, environments, and situations. Gradual exposure can help reduce fear and insecurity, which are often the root causes of aggression.

Respect Boundaries: African Greys have their own personalities, and some may not enjoy certain types of interaction. Respect the bird's boundaries and avoid forcing interaction when it shows signs of stress.

By understanding the root causes of aggression and applying appropriate training methods, you can create a more peaceful and harmonious relationship with your African Grey.

4. Separation Anxiety – Understanding and Managing Loneliness

African Greys are highly social birds and often form deep attachments to their owners. When left alone for long periods, they may experience separation anxiety, which can lead to destructive behaviors like screaming, feather plucking, and biting.

Causes of Separation Anxiety

Separation anxiety occurs when African Greys feel isolated or neglected. It can be triggered by:

- Long periods of isolation when the owner is away at work or during social events.
- Changes in routine or environment, such as moving to a new home or being introduced to new pets or people.
- Loss of a companion—either another pet or a person.

Solutions for Separation Anxiety

Managing separation anxiety requires a combination of prevention, training, and environmental changes:

Gradual Training: Begin by leaving your African Grey alone for short periods and gradually increasing the duration. This teaches the bird that being alone is not permanent and reduces the fear of separation.

Create a Comfortable Environment: Provide toys, perches, and items that can keep the bird occupied when you are away. Consider using a radio or TV to create background noise, which can help alleviate feelings of loneliness.

Ensure Mental Stimulation: Engage the bird in interactive play and training sessions before you leave. A mentally stimulated bird is less likely to resort to destructive behaviors when left alone.

Consider a Companion: In some cases, an African Grey may benefit from having a second bird as a companion. However, be mindful that not all birds get along, and introducing a new bird requires careful consideration.

Consult a Vet or Behaviorist: If separation anxiety persists, it may be helpful to consult a veterinarian or animal behaviorist who specializes in avian behavior. They can offer tailored solutions and recommendations.

Dealing with behavioral challenges in African Greys requires a combination of understanding, patience, and consistent training. These intelligent birds are more than capable of overcoming issues like boredom, aggression, feather plucking, and separation anxiety when provided with the right environment, mental stimulation, and social interaction.

By addressing the root causes of behavioral problems and implementing positive, reward-based solutions, you can enjoy a harmonious and fulfilling relationship with your African Grey. A well-trained and mentally stimulated bird will not only be a pleasure to live with but will also thrive emotionally and socially.

Chapter 10

Echoes of the Wild – The African Grey in Its Natural Habitat

In this chapter, we'll explore the African Grey parrot's natural habitat in the wild, examining the ecosystems where they live, their unique behavioral traits, and the various environmental challenges they face. Understanding the bird's natural environment is essential not only for the well-being of those kept as pets but also for the conservation efforts aimed at protecting them from the growing threats posed by habitat loss and illegal wildlife trade.

1. The Habitat of the African Grey – Understanding the Geography

Geographical Range and Distribution:
The African Grey parrot (Psittacus erithacus) is native to West and Central Africa, where it inhabits a range of forested and semi-forested regions. These areas provide the bird with the necessary resources to thrive, including a steady supply of food, nesting

sites, and shelter. The primary regions where African Greys are found in the wild include:

- West Africa: Countries like Sierra Leone, Liberia, Ivory Coast, Ghana, Nigeria, and Cameroon.
- Central Africa: The Congo Basin, particularly the rainforests of Democratic Republic of Congo (DRC), Republic of Congo, and Gabon, is home to some of the largest populations of African Greys.

African Greys are commonly found in lowland tropical rainforests, savannahs, and forest edges, but they also occasionally inhabit mangroves, riverine forests, and wooded savannas. The variation in their habitat types allows these birds to adapt to a variety of environments, though they tend to prefer areas with access to large trees for roosting and nesting, as well as a rich diversity of fruit-bearing plants.

Rainforest and Canopy Life

The African Grey's natural habitat in the rainforests is dominated by towering trees and a dense, multi-layered canopy. These birds live primarily in the middle and upper canopy layers, where they find shelter, food, and potential nesting sites. The rainforest ecosystem provides a wealth of edible items for African Greys, such as fruits, seeds, nuts, and even some flower parts.

In these forests, the birds are constantly on the move, flying from tree to tree in search of food and companionship. The dense foliage offers safety from predators and a comfortable space to forage, interact with other members of their species, and raise their young. The bird's distinctive red tail feathers make it easily identifiable in its natural habitat, contrasting sharply with the green of the forest.

While their primary residence is in the rainforests, African Greys are also found in savannahs and woodland areas at the forest edges, particularly during the dry season, when they migrate in search of more abundant food sources. These areas offer a different set of environmental challenges but still provide the resources they need to survive.

2. Social Structures and Communication in the Wild

Flocking Behavior and Social Bonds:
In their natural environment, African Greys are known for their strong social bonds. They live in small flocks that typically consist

of 2 to 30 birds. These flocks serve as a support system for the parrots, offering companionship, safety, and social interaction. The flocks are generally loose-knit, with some individuals moving in and out, while others form closer pairs or small family groups.

The size and composition of the flock can vary depending on the time of year, food availability, and the presence of predators. During the dry season, flocks tend to be smaller as food becomes scarcer, and birds are more likely to travel individually or in smaller groups to find sufficient sustenance. In the rainy season, when food sources are more abundant, larger flocks may form, allowing for greater social interactions and more opportunities for finding food together.

African Greys are highly intelligent and often engage in social behaviors that are key to their survival and well-being. Communication within flocks is paramount, and African Greys use a range of vocalizations, body language, and even mimicry to communicate with one another. These communication methods play an important role in maintaining group cohesion, signaling alarm in the presence of predators, and coordinating movements while foraging.

Vocalizations and Mimicry:

One of the most fascinating aspects of the African Grey parrot's behavior is its ability to mimic sounds and human speech. This remarkable skill is not just a party trick—it serves a purpose in the wild. African Greys use their mimicry for various forms of communication, especially when alerting others in their flock about potential dangers. For instance, an African Grey may mimic the call of a hawk or other predator, signaling the presence of danger and prompting the flock to take cover.

While African Greys are primarily known for their human speech mimicry in captivity, in the wild, their vocalizations serve more functional roles:

Alarm Calls: When threatened by predators, African Greys emit loud calls that can either send the flock into a state of alertness or prompt them to scatter to safety. These calls are often high-pitched, shrill, and sharp, designed to catch the attention of other members of the flock.

Social Calls: African Greys also use softer calls to stay in touch with other members of the flock while foraging or moving between trees. These calls help maintain the group's cohesion, ensuring that the birds don't become too dispersed.

Mimicry of Other Species: In addition to their alarm calls, African Greys can mimic the sounds of other animals, including the calls of other bird species, primates, and even environmental sounds like wind or rain. This ability can help them blend in with the surrounding environment or confuse potential predators.

3. Diet and Foraging in the Wild

Food Sources and Feeding Habits:
African Greys are omnivores, and their diet in the wild is highly varied. They primarily feed on a combination of fruits, seeds, nuts, berries, and occasionally insects or other small animals. The rich diversity of the rainforest provides an abundant supply of food, allowing African Greys to maintain a well-rounded diet.

Fruits and Seeds: African Greys are known to feed on a variety of tropical fruits such as figs, palm fruits, and berries, as well as seeds from a range of trees. They have a keen ability to identify edible fruit and seed-bearing plants, and their sharp beaks are well-suited to cracking open nuts and extracting seeds.

Nuts: Nuts, including palm nuts and Brazil nuts, form an important part of the African Grey's diet. These nuts are a great source of fat and protein, and the birds are adept at using their powerful beaks to crack them open.

Flowers and Leaves: Although not a primary food source, African Greys occasionally forage on flowers and leaf buds. These provide essential vitamins and minerals, especially when fruits and seeds are scarce.

Insects and Small Creatures: While not a large part of their diet, African Greys do supplement their meals with insects, larvae, and occasionally small vertebrates such as lizards. This provides them with the protein necessary for growth and health.

The African Grey's foraging behavior is highly sophisticated. They often work in pairs or small groups to search for food, communicating with one another as they forage. This cooperative behavior allows them to find food more efficiently, and it helps strengthen the social bonds within the flock.

Nesting and Reproduction:

In the wild, African Greys are cavity nesters. They seek out large trees with suitable hollow cavities where they can build their nests. These cavities provide a safe and secure environment for raising young, protecting them from predators and harsh environmental conditions.

African Greys typically lay two to four eggs during the breeding season, with the female incubating the eggs for around 30 days. The parents are highly attentive, with the male often helping to bring food to the female while she is incubating the eggs. After hatching, the chicks are completely dependent on their parents for food and warmth for the first few weeks.

The parents feed their young by regurgitating food directly into their mouths. As the chicks grow, they gradually become more independent, eventually learning to fly and forage on their own. By the time they reach 6 months of age, the young African Greys are usually able to leave the nest and join the rest of the flock in search of food and social interaction.

4. Predators and Threats in the Wild

Natural Predators:

Despite their impressive intelligence and ability to communicate, African Greys face numerous predators in the wild. These include:

Birds of Prey: Raptors such as hawks, eagles, and falcons are among the most dangerous predators of African Greys. These birds of prey have sharp talons and keen eyesight, making them well-equipped to capture and kill parrots.

Snakes: Certain species of snakes in the African rainforest, including tree-dwelling pythons, pose a significant threat to African Greys, particularly when they are nesting in tree cavities.

Mammals: Larger predators, including monkeys, wildcats, and even baboons, sometimes pose a danger to African Greys, especially if they come across the birds while foraging or nesting.

Despite these threats, African Greys are quite adept at using their intelligence to evade predators. Their ability to mimic sounds, including the calls of predators, allows them to remain hidden and protected when danger is near. Additionally, their quick flight capabilities and agility in the trees provide an escape route when a predator approaches.

Human-Induced Threats:

The most significant threats to African Greys, however, come from human activities. These include:

Habitat Destruction: Deforestation, largely driven by logging, agriculture, and urban expansion, has led to the loss of vast portions of the African Grey's natural habitat. The destruction of tropical rainforests and the encroachment on savannahs has drastically reduced the available territory for these birds, leaving them increasingly vulnerable to extinction.

Illegal Pet Trade: The African Grey is one of the most trafficked bird species in the world. Due to their beauty, intelligence, and ability to mimic human speech, African Greys are highly sought after in the illegal pet trade. This has led to the decimation of wild populations, with many birds being captured and sold for profit, often at the expense of the species' survival in the wild.

Climate Change: Changes in climate patterns can also have a profound impact on African Greys. Shifts in rainfall patterns, temperature, and food availability can affect their ability to find resources and may force them to migrate to unfamiliar areas, further stressing their already vulnerable populations.

The African Grey parrot, with its striking intelligence and emotional depth, is a creature that carries with it the echoes of its wild heritage. While these birds have adapted to life in captivity, their natural habitat offers invaluable insights into their behavior, social structures, and ecological needs.

The rainforest and savannahs of West and Central Africa are more than just the backdrop for their survival—they are integral to understanding what makes the African Grey unique. From their complex vocalizations and foraging habits to their social interactions and nesting behaviors, the African Grey's existence in the wild is a testament to the resilience and adaptability of this remarkable species.

However, with increasing environmental threats, including habitat destruction and illegal wildlife trade, the future of the African Grey in the wild is uncertain. Understanding the bird's natural environment is crucial for conservation efforts aimed at preserving this iconic species for generations to come. As we continue to learn from and care for these incredible creatures, we must also work toward protecting the wild places they call home, ensuring that the African Grey can continue to echo through the rainforests and savannas of Africa.

Conclusion

The African Grey parrot (Psittacus erithacus) is undoubtedly one of the most captivating bird species on the planet, renowned not only for its breathtaking beauty but also for its exceptional cognitive abilities, complex social behavior, and emotional intelligence. As we have explored throughout this discussion, the African Grey is a creature of many dimensions, seamlessly blending the worlds of nature, intelligence, and companionship. This final conclusion will reflect on the key aspects of this bird, synthesizing the knowledge shared to underscore the importance of understanding and caring for the African Grey in both wild and domestic settings.

The Unrivaled Intelligence of the African Grey

When it comes to intelligence, few animals can rival the African Grey parrot. Studies have shown that these birds possess cognitive abilities that are on par with some of the most advanced non-human animals. Their capacity for problem-solving, tool use, self-awareness, and theory of mind (the ability to attribute mental states to others) sets them apart as truly remarkable creatures.

African Greys have been shown to understand concepts like cause and effect, numbers, and even shapes and colors.

The bird's ability to mimic human speech is not just a display of entertainment; it is a reflection of the bird's sophisticated auditory processing and memory capacity. The African Grey does not simply repeat words but understands their meanings in context, demonstrating an advanced level of comprehension. This capacity for mimicry and speech, coupled with their social intelligence, enables them to engage in complex interactions with humans and other animals.

This intelligence is not only an interesting feature of the African Grey but also plays an important role in its survival and social structures in the wild. In the dense African rainforests, where resources can be scarce and threats from predators loom large, the ability to adapt, communicate effectively, and solve problems is critical. Their mental faculties allow them to navigate complex environments, find food, and interact with other members of their species in meaningful ways.

The Deep Emotional Bond Between African Greys and Humans

One of the most striking features of the African Grey parrot is its deep emotional sensitivity. Unlike many other birds, African Greys form strong emotional bonds with their human caretakers, displaying attachment behaviors and complex emotions such as joy, fear, sadness, and affection.

This emotional depth makes African Greys especially unique as companion animals. They do not simply mimic human speech; they respond to the emotions of their human caregivers, offering comfort in times of distress and expressing joy in moments of shared happiness. These emotional exchanges, though sometimes subtle, form the basis of the bonds between African Greys and humans. The bird's empathy is often seen in its ability to sense the emotional states of its owners, responding with empathy and understanding.

This deep connection, however, also means that African Greys are not just simple pets—they are emotionally complex beings that require constant mental stimulation, social interaction, and a sense of security. The absence of these elements can lead to significant psychological distress, such as boredom, depression, and even self-destructive behaviors. Their emotional needs are as important as their intellectual ones, requiring conscientious care and attention from their human companions.

Environmental Adaptability: From Wild to Home

One of the most remarkable traits of the African Grey parrot is its adaptability. Whether in the wild or in domestic settings, the bird demonstrates an incredible ability to adjust to different environments. In the wild, African Greys navigate the vast African rainforests and savannahs, foraging for food, evading predators, and forming intricate social structures. Their intelligence and emotional sensitivity enable them to thrive in complex ecosystems, where they must constantly adapt to shifting resources and environmental challenges.

In captivity, African Greys can also adapt to human homes, as long as their environmental needs are met. They require a habitat that mimics their natural environment as closely as possible, with access to mental stimulation, social interaction, and physical activity. These birds are highly social and require a stimulating environment that challenges their intellect. If these needs are met, the African Grey can live a long, happy, and healthy life as a companion animal.

This adaptability, however, should not be mistaken for simplicity. While African Greys are capable of adjusting to a variety of living conditions, their needs are specific and should not be overlooked. They require a commitment of time, effort, and understanding from their caregivers. Their intellectual and emotional complexity makes them more than just a pet; they are lifelong companions that need to be nurtured, respected, and cared for throughout their lives.

Conservation Challenges and Ethical Considerations

While the African Grey parrot is admired for its intelligence and beauty, it faces significant challenges in the wild. One of the most pressing threats to the species is habitat loss. The vast rainforests and savannas of Africa, which provide the necessary resources for African Greys to survive, are rapidly disappearing due to deforestation, logging, agriculture, and urban expansion. As the African Grey's natural habitat is destroyed, these birds are forced into smaller, fragmented areas, where they face increased competition for resources and greater vulnerability to predators.

In addition to habitat loss, the African Grey is also heavily impacted by the illegal pet trade. Due to their intelligence, striking appearance, and ability to mimic human speech, African Greys are highly sought after in the international pet market. This has led to widespread poaching, with birds being captured and sold illegally, often at great cost to wild populations. The African Grey is listed as vulnerable by the International Union for Conservation of Nature (IUCN), and its population continues to decline, driven in part by human-induced pressures.

Efforts to conserve the African Grey parrot are ongoing, but more needs to be done to protect their habitats and curb illegal trafficking. This includes enforcing stricter regulations on the wildlife trade, protecting critical rainforest and savannah habitats, and promoting awareness about the ethical considerations of keeping African Greys as pets. Ethical breeding programs and conservation efforts that protect both wild and captive African Greys are essential for ensuring the species' survival.

The African Grey as a Lifelong Companion

When considering the African Grey as a pet, it is crucial to understand the commitment required to care for such an intelligent and emotionally complex animal. These birds are not suitable for everyone. They require a significant investment of time, energy, and resources to ensure they remain mentally and emotionally healthy. The mental stimulation, social interaction, and emotional support they require are not optional; they are essential for their well-being.

For those who are prepared for the responsibility, however, the rewards of having an African Grey as a companion can be immense. The bird's capacity for speech and mimicry is fascinating, and the emotional bond that forms between the bird and its human caregivers is deeply rewarding. Many African Grey owners report the joy of hearing their birds speak and perform tricks, as well as the unique companionship that only an intelligent, affectionate bird can offer.

The African Grey is a lifelong commitment, requiring careful attention to diet, mental health, physical activity, and social needs. They thrive in environments where they are challenged intellectually and socially, and they need to be part of the family, interacting with their caregivers regularly. Those who commit to the care of an African Grey will find that it is a deeply fulfilling experience—one that offers the opportunity to witness firsthand the remarkable intelligence, emotional depth, and beauty of this extraordinary bird.

The African Grey parrot is a creature of extraordinary beauty, intelligence, and emotional depth. It is a bird that captivates us not only with its striking appearance but also with its remarkable abilities. From its advanced cognitive skills and mimicry to its deep emotional bonds with humans, the African Grey is a testament to the complexity of animal behavior and the remarkable capacity for connection across species.

However, the African Grey is also a species facing significant challenges in the wild, from habitat loss to the illegal pet trade. It is essential that we continue to raise awareness about the plight of the African Grey and work toward conservation and ethical breeding practices to protect them for future generations.

www.ingramcontent.com/pod-product-compliance
Ingram Content Group UK Ltd.
Pitfield, Milton Keynes, MK11 3LW, UK
UKHW021452020126
9863UKWH00013B/153